A Swim for Dear Life

The True Story of a Titanic Survivor

Brian Edwards

£9.95

Dedication.

For Verbena
with my thanks

ISBN 1-902074-01-7

First Edition June 1998
© B.L.Edwards.

The publishers would like to thank Dave Cook and all the staff of W. E. Baxters Ltd.,
Roger Colbourne Editorial and Research Services for proof reading this book and
Julie Wood for her historical advice and guidance.

Published by

GORDONS PUBLISHING.

7 Ravenshead Close,
Selsdon,
South Croydon,
Surrey,
CR2 8RL
A division of   **GORDONS MEDALS Ltd.**

Contents

Plates

Prologue

Outside Hessle, just to the north of the Humber Bridge, stands Tranby House, set in its own grounds. Now part of the Hessle Secondary School, its last private owner was my great uncle, Algernon Henry Barkworth.

The Barkworths were merchants from Hull, where in the eighteenth century John Barkworth, Algy's great grandfather, had built up a timber and shipping business. Dealing first in 'junk' timber and operating from offices in Dock Street, he eventually expanded his business, hired out and maintained his own ships and imported fine timber and mahogany. Unconfirmed family tradition suggests that he may also have been involved in the shipment of slaves on the outward voyages. Be that as it may, he and his eldest son, also John, each had fifteen children and together built up a minor dynasty, which was, however, not to survive as a coherent whole much beyond the third generation.

In keeping with his improved status, John Barkworth senior, by now a Board Member of the Honourable East India Company, purchased a site outside Hessle, where in 1805 he built Tranby House. The House passed via his widow, Elizabeth, to John Barkworth junior, who in due course passed it, also via his widow, Emma, to his second son Henry Boulderson Barkworth.

By 1912, when this tale begins, Henry Barkworth had been dead fourteen years and once again it was the widow, Catherine Hester, who occupied Tranby House. With her lived Algy, her younger son, and Evelyn, her unmarried daughter.

The year was to be one of mixed fortunes for the Barkworth family; it opened with the death of my grandmother, Algy's sister in law, after a protracted illness. Two months later Algy decided to undertake a journey to New York by White Star Line. It was to be the most memorable journey of his life.

A. H. Barkworth J.P.

4

A Swim for Dear Life.

At the beginning of 1912 newspapers and magazines were carrying articles and advertisements which heralded the imminent completion of what was to be the largest and most luxurious ocean liner in the world. The Titanic was scheduled to make its first passenger trip, sailing from Southampton on Wednesday 10th April. On impulse Algernon Barkworth booked his passage *largely out of curiosity as to what she was like'*. He was to travel first class and made plans to stay one month in America.

Great Uncle Algy was one of four children and the younger of two brothers.He was also a bachelor and had continued to live at Tranby House, Hessle, with his mother and elder sister since his father died in 1898; he would be forty eight in June. Although educated at Eton and Oxford and having been trained in the law, he does not seem to have practised, but satisfied what legal aspirations he may have had by sitting on the local Bench as a JP.

His father and his brother both shared an interest in horses and hunting, but Algy's passion was for things mechanical, which he mainly indulged by the purchase of cars and motorcycles, including a large American roadster nicknamed 'Dixie'. He normally showed a modest disposition so that one of his colleagues on the Bench described him as a 'natural gentleman', but if need arose he could show an obstinate determination, as was demonstrated by the report which appeared in the Hull Daily Mail of the 20th May 1900....

"In the Queen's Bench Division today an action was heard which was brought by Mr Algernon Barkworth of Tranby, Hessle, near Hull, against a London motorcar company for alleged breach of contract.
"It appeared that in 1898 the plaintiff ordered an Orient Express car for £201 and paid a deposit of £75. After several trials, plaintiff was not satisfied, and agreed to take a Barriere tricycle, the price being 75 Guineas.This, when delivered, was not painted as required and did not work satisfactorily, and had to be sent back for repairs. It was then arranged that a new tricycle should be sent, but the plaintiff said, when he saw it, that it was an old one, and he refused to accept it.
"The jury found for the plaintiff for £89 and costs".

The voyage in the Titanic would not be his first trip to sea. Seven years before, his sister in law had become ill and the doctors had advised a long sea voyage. His brother Edmund booked a passage on the SS Tangariro for New Zealand and embarked at Tilbury with Ada, their three children and the governess. Algy decided to travel with them as far as Capetown. Sadly that was where the voyage ended, as Ada became seriously ill and they returned from South Africa by the first available boat. In February, only two months before Titanic sailed, Algy had been down to attend her funeral at Piddletrenthide in Dorset, where she had died after a long illness.

There was an unaccustomed bustle in the household on the morning of Tuesday 9th April with last minute packing and labelling of bags and cabin trunk. To pack for the voyage was by no means easy. At a minimum one would require three or four suits, a city suit for New York, a tweed for day wear on the ship and informal occasions onshore, a dinner suit for evening wear with at least sufficient stiff boiled shirts to last the voyage, during which the first class passengers were expected to dress for dinner. Once in America, the land of the automobile, there would be motoring to consider; besides, spring was not far advanced and the weather had been so blustery on the previous week that the Boat Race had had to be rerun, after the Oxford and Cambridge boats had each foundered in rough water. A Norfolk jacket, knickerbockers and thick worsted stockings were sure to be needed and, of course, a travelling rug.

One did not travel light in the days before man made fibres and plastics, when men's clothes and underclothes, the latter long and substantial, were all wool and when bags and suitcases were of leather. Of course a gentleman seldom carried his own luggage and any sympathy must go to the servants, porters and stewards who would have to heave it around on the journey from Hessle to his first class stateroom in 'Titanic'.

As he left that morning for London and Southampton, Algy made a decision that he would afterwards consider to be one of the most crucial of his life - he decided to take with him his long fur coat.

RMS Titanic had berthed at Southampton just before midnight on the previous Wednesday, since when she had been storing, victualling and taking on staff ready to receive her first passengers.

WHITE STAR LINER TITANIC.
LENGTH 882 ft. 6 ins.   BREADTH 92 ft. 6 ins   45,000 TONNAGE.
SAILED FROM SOUTHAMPTON ON HER ILL-FATED MAIDEN VOYAGE ON APRIL 10TH, 1912, CARRYING 2,350 PASSENGERS AND CREW. STRUCK AN ICEBERG
OFF THE COAST OF NEWFOUNDLAND, PERISHED ON SUNDAY NIGHT APRIL 14TH, 1912.

Taking on stores was a huge undertaking akin to equipping a large first class hotel from scratch. On this occasion it not only had to be completed in 5 days, but it also took place over Easter. LInen stores alone comprised an exhaustive list from 4,000 aprons and 15,000 single sheets to 8,000 bath towels, and even then there were a further 40,000 miscellaneous items unspecified. The list of crockery and tableware included everything one could imagine, from 12,000 dinner plates to 1,500 champagne glasses, and some items less imaginable, such as 400 pairs of asparagus tongs. To go with the tongs there were 800 bundles of fresh asparagus, while about 125,000 lbs of meat and fish were matched by 40 tons of potatoes, to be washed down by a choice from 20,000 bottles of beer and 1500 of wine. The bakers had 200 barrels of flour and to go with their baking there were 6,000 lbs of butter and more than a thousand lbs of jams. These quantities reflect that there were over 2,000 passengers and crew to feed on a voyage of six days in a liner that was designed to be the largest and most luxurious afloat.

The boat train for first class passengers left Waterloo at 9.45 on the morning of 10th April and was not due at the dockside until 11.30. This was only half an hour before the ship was scheduled to sail. A number of passengers however chose to make their own arrangements and boarded earlier. First aboard had been Bruce Ismay, President of the White Star Line, who was to travel in the ship for its maiden voyage and had stayed overnight in the Great Western Hotel. He brought with him his family, who were not travelling but were to be shown around his superb new vessel. From his position on the passenger list, Algy seems to have been amongst those who chose to embark independently and to avoid the last-minute crowd on the dockside. Since each steward minded eight or so cabins, there was the mutual advantage that the early arrivals could be unpacked and settled in their staterooms before the rush began. It also allowed time to find one's way around the ship.

Algy was immediately struck by the *'magnificence of the appointments'*, as indeed were most of his fellow passengers in the first class accommodation. Each of the cabins, known as staterooms, had its own decor which varied in style from Tudor to contemporary, while for those prepared to pay there were suites or adjoining rooms for family or servants. The incoming passenger, that day, came aboard on the port side of the ship through an entrance leading to the main, or grand, staircase, which served the first class staterooms as well as their reception and dining rooms. It reached to a depth of 60 ft from the boat deck, where it was capped by an ornate glass dome just forward of the second funnel. It ran down through the main foyer, which led in turn to a main lounge furnished in elegant contemporary Edwardian fashion, then down a further four decks, from where it also gave access to the swimming pool, the squash court and the turkish bath. The style of the staircase, being heavily panelled and carved, was attributed to a combination of William and Mary and Louis XIV - historically at least contemporaries.

There was a second staircase for first class passengers, only marginally less grand and also capped by a glass dome. This was just forward of the after funnel and served only three decks, including the first class smoking room, intended for men only and furnished in appropriate club style with green leather chairs, and the 'a la carte' restaurant one deck down, where for an extra cost you could dine alone or entertain. This staircase also provided easier access to a number of staterooms in the after part of the first class accommodation. Apart from these vertical walkways, there was a crew staircase and also three lifts. Movement fore and aft was possible for most of the length of the ship on the boat deck, the promenade decks and by a wide corridor down on E deck, known to the officers as Park Lane and to the crew as Scotland Road.

Finding one's way around any vessel, let alone one as vast as 'Titanic', is not easy. Algy's cabin, or stateroom, was Number A 23, on the starboard side of A Deck and just below the Boatdeck. In his first tentative exploration, he could not fail to find the smoking room and the main lounge, both of which were on the same level as his state room. The main lounge stretched across the ship and had windows opening on to the promenade decks. There were other facilities at these levels of less immediate interest to a confirmed bachelor of forty eight, including a writing and reading room to which the ladies were expected to retire but, we are told, rarely did.

For the younger set there was a 'cafe parisienne', furnished in wickerwork and decorated with trellis and palms, while up in the superstructure at boatdeck level, there was an up to date gymnasium, where the fitness enthusiast could work out on rowing or cycling machines, keep riding muscles in trim on mechanical horses, tone up on weight apparatus or knock hell out of the mechanical equivalent of a punch bag. One suspects that Algy's interest in the apparatus would have been in the mechanics rather than the use. For exercise the promenade would have sufficed.

In 1912 trains ran to time, even in the South. Boat trains arrived and deposited their passengers who streamed up their allotted gangways - depending on whether they were travelling first class, second class or steerage - while baggage was lifted on board by crane. Punctually at midday 'Titanic' slipped from the dockside and began to nose ahead, shepherded by five tugs. Most people enjoy the spectacle of other people at work and the passengers crowding the rails got their money's worth, not all of it scheduled. Once the tugs were buttoned on there was the excitement of all wires being let go at once and being run ashore by the dockers who swarmed along the wharf. Ahead of 'Titanic' was a smaller American liner 'New York', berthed alongside, unmanned and temporarily out of service because of a coal strike. As the huge liner passed, the suction it created caused the smaller ship to swing out and its stern wires parted with a series of loud reports. Captain Smith on the bridge of 'Titanic' reacted quickly and went astern on the engines so that his ship went slowly back into the dock, while a tug got wires onto 'New York' and averted a collision. By the time all was secured and it was safe to proceed, sailing had been delayed by over an hour and it was time for the passengers to go down to lunch.

As she came out of Southampton Water the liner turned east down the Solent then south to the Nab lightship, where she dropped the pilot. Passengers who did not linger over lunch and were on deck to watch him climb down the jacob's ladder into the pilot boat, which was bouncing around in the swell, could be forgiven for feeling comfortably secure in the safety of their vast vessel, said to be unsinkable because of its system of watertight compartments, controlled from the bridge at a touch of a button .

The first port of call before the Atlantic crossing was Cherbourg, where the ship was to pick up passengers who were travelling down by train from Paris. The crossing was a short hop of about 70 miles from the Nab, allowing those already aboard time to complete settling in and to take tea in the main lounge or the palm court. Algy scribbled a note to his brother, Edmund, on a postcard, the front of which held a dramatic portrayal of either the 'Titanic' or her sister ship the 'Olympic', in whichever it was sold....

Have made a good start and are nearing Cherbourg. Everything is <u>most</u> magnificent and impossible to describe. Hope the sale goes well. Just passed St Albans....

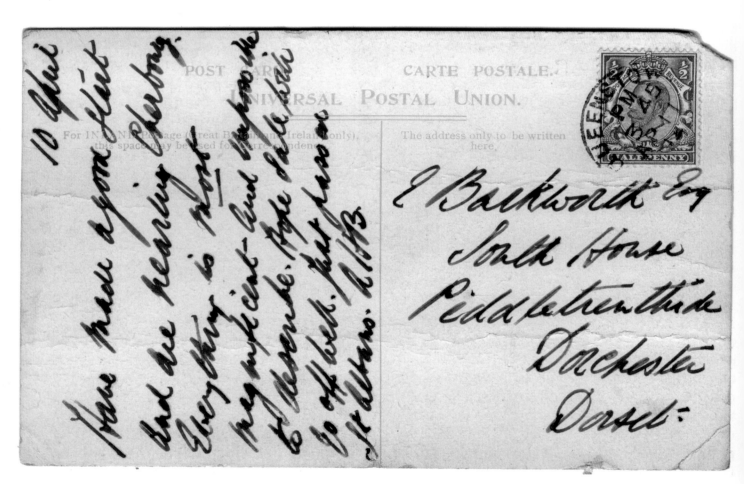

Because of the delay in leaving Southampton the ship did not drop anchor in Cherbourg roadstead until after sunset, by which time it was dark and many passengers were already changing for dinner. Those who were on deck to watch the arrival saw little but the shadow of the low lying land and the twinkling lights of the port. By contrast, those on the two tenders bringing off the new passengers had a superb impression of the enormous bulk of 'Titanic', ablaze with light from stem to stern. Loading was completed in an hour and a half. The anchor was hauled in and with three blasts of her siren she sailed westward towards Ireland for her final landfall, leaving the last reluctant diners to hurry down to the dining room on D Deck, a splendid room decorated in Jacobean style, where over 500 diners could be served at a sitting. Before that Algy had penned a further card to his niece Dorothy....

Just arriving at Cherbourg. Rather stormy and cold but in my <u>room</u> you would hardly know the engines were going. We arrive Queenstown tomorrow but then it is all to try...

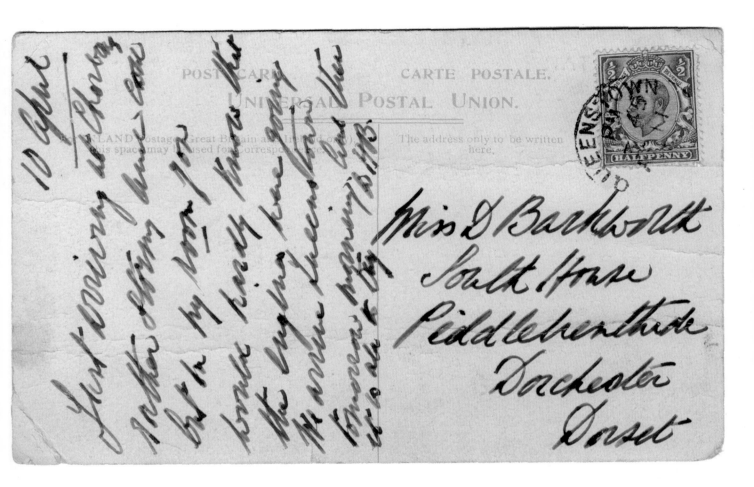

The crossing was smooth enough to allow for a good night's sleep and a hearty breakfast before anchoring two miles off Queenstown shortly after 'elevenses'. Passengers and mail were ferried out by paddle steamer and were brought inboard through double doors on E Deck, while local entrepeneurs in smaller boats brought off goods to trade with gullible buyers. When the paddle boats left they took with them the handful of passengers who had paid £4 to travel as far as Queenstown and who now disembarked, watched by those 'rubber-necking' above and taking a last look at the green landscape; they also took Algy's postcards for posting ashore. Then it was lunchtime again, but those who remained on deck for a little longer, as 'Titanic' steamed out into the Atlantic, could have heard the thin wail of Irish pipes floating up from the third class accommodation, where a homesick emigrant was playing 'Erin's Lament'.

The arrival and departure of a luxury liner was dictated as much by mealtimes as by tides and three excellent square meals a day continued to be the framework for life aboard. The sea remained calm and the ship gathered speed, while published bulletins kept passengers informed of the distance travelled over the previous twenty four hours. Time passed easily between meals. For those in need of entertainment the orchestra worked in groups, operating as strolling minstrels, playing light music as a trio in the palm court or giving full orchestral recitals in the lounge.

The social set was bright, even brilliant. Apart from the Astors, the Duff Coopers and the Countess of Rothes, there was an imposing selection of successful and rich business magnates and bankers, with a sprinkling of millionaires, many travelling with their families and wives, who at dinner would appear in a glitter of jewelry. Then there were a knight or two, a congressman, a member of parliament, a master of foxhounds, a tennis player, a painter, a couple of writers, and a well known journalist called William Stead. The latter was also a medium and an evangelist, as well as being a newspaper editor, and had published a number of items about disasters at sea. Essentially it was a cosmopolitan gathering with a sprinkling of diplomats or military aides and a number of bright young things, several on honeymoon, all adding to the glamour of the occasion.

Postcard sent to Algy's brother

The number of first class passengers on board meant that there were new people to meet each day, whether strolling on the boat or promenade decks, playing a 'rubber' of bridge in the smoking room, chatting over a drink in the palm court or cafe parisienne, or just meeting on the staircase. For those with more solitary tastes there was a well-stocked library and all the most recent magazines, including the Illustrated London News with some entertaining pictures of the foundering of the Oxford and Cambridge boats.

Presiding over the wellbeing of ship and passengers, whether professional or social, was the smart and immensely reassuring figure of the Captain of 'Titanic'; Captain Edward Smith, described by one as a 'giant of a seaman', was the senior and most experienced captain of the White Star Line and the natural choice to take this great new ship on her maiden voyage.

The morning of Sunday 14th April, the fourth day out from Queenstown and the fifth from Southampton, started much like any other except that after breakfast the first class dining room was rigged for church. For people brought up in the Victorian or Edwardian era religious attendance was an important matter of routine. The Barkworth households at Tranby and Piddletrenthide were accustomed to hold daily prayers in their own dining rooms, attended by family and servants, and Algy would have found the arrangements on board logical. On this Sunday morning the hymns included 'Oh God our help in ages past' and the prayers included one for 'those in peril on the sea'. Some people were later to attribute a prescience of doom to these choices, which are however typical of any such service at sea. Besides, we are told that the hymn was a favourite of Mr Hartley the bandmaster.

In addition to attendance at church there was one other duty learnt at an early age by any small boy sent to boarding school and that was to write home each Sunday. However, this ship had a Marconi room equipped with wireless, which enabled messages to be passed from ship to shore. Algy was in tune with the advances of science and instead of writing a letter sent a wireless message to his mother at Tranby, of which the text read simply "*All Well - Algy*". Other passengers had the same idea so that John Phillips, the senior wireless operator, was kept busy till late in the evening clearing the messages through the shore station at Cape Race. This did not prevent him from receiving a number of ice warnings which were passed on to the bridge.

Postcard sent to Algy's Niece

During the day the throb of 'Titanic's' turbines had continued uninterrupted and, in the calm sea conditions which persisted, the ship made such good time that there was a rumour that on the following day they would run up to full power and perhaps even set a crossing record. Rumours of ice packs drifting down into the shipping lane had also reached the passengers and as if to confirm these there was a marked drop in temperature. Those taking exercise on the upper decks wrapped up well but there was no sign of any slackening of the ship's speed, nor was there any apparent concern.

After dinner most first class passengers, dressed in their finery, attended the usual orchestral recital in the main lounge, before filtering off to their staterooms to turn in. Algy stayed up late in the smoking room, where the men were sitting around chatting in groups, reading, or just having a nightcap. Some were playing bridge, the chief steward apparently having been persuaded to waive the normal rule enforced by the White Star Line, which forbade the playing of cards on Sunday. Algy, brought up in a house which was taught to regard the Bible as the only proper book to be read on Sunday, may have been surprised but does not appear to have been driven to bed by this breach of Lord's Day observance. If he had any sense of vicarious enjoyment then he would have seen what was to follow as retribution.

At about twenty minutes to midnight those in the smoking room felt a jolt, which caused the ship to sway as if it had been brought alongside some jetty too fast. It was immediately apparent that the rhythm of the engines had changed and very shortly they stopped altogether. A startled steward and one of the passengers were first out of the door and on deck, others followed. Somebody called out that the ship had hit an iceberg but for those behind there was nothing to be seen and it was decidedly cold. People filtered back into the smoking room, where the cards enthusiasts were still at play, and one of the stewards was sent off to find out what was going on.

Time passed and he did not return, but one or two passengers came in with tales of ice on the ship up in the bows. Curiosity drove Algy and a number of others to investigate and they hurried up the enclosed promenade deck to a position under the bridge, from where they could look through the windows across to the foc'sle and down into the welldeck. They saw plenty of powdered ice around and watched some of the crew and steerage passengers skylarking and playing football with chunks of ice.

Meanwhile the number on deck had grown, as those who had been in their cabins arrived in a motley assortment of clothes or dressing gowns to discover what was happening. Many found it too cold and drifted down the grand staircase into the foyer below to await developments. Algy noticed the journalist William Stead who was one of the last to arrive and who announced that, as nothing seemed to be happening, he was returning to his stateroom to read.

Captain Smith went on an inspection of the fore part of the ship with Thomas Andrews, the ship's designer and the representative on board of Harland and Wolff, builders of 'Titanic'. He returned to the bridge just after midnight, passing through the foyer without speaking to the passengers gathered there. Watertight doors had been closed but, after a brief discussion with Mr Andrews, he knew that the number of compartments flooding meant that the ship would inevitably sink. At 1205 therefore, twenty five minutes after the collision, he gave instructions for lifeboats to be uncovered and for officers off watch to be called, including Second Officer Charles Lightoller. The First Officer was ordered to muster the passengers. Captain Smith then walked the short distance to the wireless shack and gave instructions to John Phillips and Harold Bride, assistant wireless operator, for sending out a distress call.

In some respects 'Titanic' was better equipped for communication with other ships than with its own passengers and crew. There seems to have been no internal speaker system and the fifty line telephone exchange does not feature in reports on the events of that night. For conning the ship there were voice pipes and the engine room telegraphs, while for upper deck work there were speaking trumpets. To call the hungry to meals a bugler went round between decks but all other information had to be delivered by hand or word of mouth. The ship had signed on no less than fifteen bellboys to carry messages in the first class accommodation. The principal channel of communication with passengers was through the stewards but to brief the stewards themselves was difficult enough. The groups which Algy had left playing cards in the smoking room, were still enjoying their game until an officer looked in and called, "Men, get on your life jackets; there's trouble ahead !"

Slowly the news filtered down but reactions were often slow, due to a persistent belief that the ship was unsinkable, compounded by a determination not to alarm the passengers. Algy got the message by chance from the mouth of the Captain himself :-

' I saw Captain Smith surrounded by a group of crying ladies asking him many questions. "Go back to your cabins,ladies," he said, "put on your life jackets and come back to the boatdeck. I assure you there is no danger". I thought that sounded rather bad, myself.'

This was the last time that Algy remembered seeing the Captain, who returned in due course to the bridge while Algy went straight to his stateroom *'to change'*. Once there he does not seem to have done much changing but, still wearing his stiff dress shirt, he got out his life jacket and tied it over his suit. Then, picking up his long fur coat, he put it on over the top and climbed back up to the boatdeck, where the ships officers had started to load the boats.

There seemed to him to be no panic and loading of women and children was proceeding in a fairly leisurely way. The men had been told to stand back, and those with families delivered them to the boats and then joined the others standing amidships. Manhood was reached that night at the age of 13 or 14 depending on which ship's officer was conducting the loading.

Sometimes there was a brief scene when a woman grew hysterical and declined to enter a boat, or when a man lost his cool and tried to push his way in. The officers were firm with both, and women were put in or men pulled out as appropriate. A few of the women had their way and stayed in the ship with their husbands.

The orchestra, which had been playing in the foyer where people had first gathered, now moved up onto the boatdeck and set up by the entrance to the staircase on the port side of the ship. It played a selection of songs, ragtime and waltzes, which eased the mood and helped to maintain calm as people waited.

At 1245, over an hour after the iceberg had been struck, the first boat was lowered and almost simultaneously those on deck were startled by a rocket which shot up from the bridge and cast a brilliant white light over the scene. As each distress rocket was followed by another even the most optimistic began to realise that the situation was indeed serious. The boats were lowered at intervals as they were filled. At times there was a shortage of women and children, as second class and steerage passengers failed to find their way to the boatdeck in the first class areas, or in some cases were denied access. Sometimes a man who was in the right place was allowed aboard, but some boats were lowered half or three quarters full and were told to lie off the ship.

Helping to load the boats were a number of passengers, including Bruce Ismay in his carpet slippers, who at times was more hindrance than help, it not being clear whether he was acting as owner, crew or passenger. There was also a US colonel turned writer named Archibald Gracie, who was on holiday to recuperate from his most recent book. Mostly the men were standing quietly in groups or on their own. Jack Thayer, the seventeen year old son of a vice president of the Pennsylvania Railroad and travelling with his parents, was chatting with a new found friend. Elsewhere his mother was waiting for the last of the sixteen ship's lifeboats to be loaded. Eventually it left the ship at 1.55. and only the collapsible Engelhardt boats remained. Indeed one of these had already left carrying Bruce Ismay, who with questionable motive had climbed into the boat at the last moment as it was lowered.

Algy had been standing around for the best part of an hour and decided at some point to go to his stateroom, as he tells us in a report he made later when asked about the band :-

"I returned to my cabin to try to get some things, but found the door locked. The band at that time was playing a waltz tune, but when I returned from the cabin and passed the place where the band had been stationed their instruments were thrown down and the members were nowhere to be seen. This was some time before I left the ship; whether the band commenced to play again I cannot say for they were on the opposite side of the ship to that which I climbed over. They might have returned to their instruments... I will never forget the jarring notes of that waltz."

[This report differs from others which record that the band played on and ended its brave performance with a hymn tune, the identity of which is also a subject of continued debate. Whatever the details, the courage shown and the contribution made by Mr Hartley and his musicians, none of whom were saved, is nowhere disputed.]

By now time was running out, with conditions worsening by the minute. The ship was down by the bows and the angle grew steeper. Somehow one of the collapsibles was fitted into the falls and was lowered. It was then 2.05. The remaining two boats were maddeningly inaccessible, being stowed on top of the officers' quarters behind the bridge. Second Officer Lightoller and other members of the crew were trying to free the lashings to get the boats down to the davits below. Colonel Gracie lent them his penknife. Harold Bride came out from the wireless shack to lend a hand. By the time they had slid them down oars to the boatdeck, it was too late to get either to the falls. Boat A was still partially collapsed and Boat B was upside down. Then at 2.15 the sea came over the bridge in a wave.

Algy, who was on the starboard side of the boatdeck and not far away, tells his own story;

"After all the boats had gone everybody seemed to be waiting for death on the doomed ship. I, however, determined to leave the ship and make a fight for my life in the water. I climbed onto the top rail on the boatdeck and, getting over, hung suspended by the side of the ship over the sea with one hand. I should say the distance to the water was about 30 feet now, for the vessel had such a list that I thought she was going to turn turtle. She had also sunk considerably in the water, for ordinarily the distance to the water would have been seventy feet."

The upturned collapsable lifeboat B, adrift in the Atlantic

" I hesitated for a few moments before dropping, for the sea seemed to be full of chairs and other wreckage thrown overboard by the passengers, and I thought that I might hurt myself. Fancy thinking of such a thing at such a time. It has occurred to me that it was dangerous to have dropped down the side of the vessel for fear she might have sunk quickly, and that it might have been better to jump clear. How far I fell I cannot tell, and I swallowed no end of salt water."

"When I came to the surface I swam as hard as I could go to get away from the suction I expected would be created by the sinking of such a large vessel. I am a good swimmer, and after swimming for a considerable distance in the icy cold water, I managed to get hold of a piece of wreckage, which I got under my arms. This supported me somewhat, and I was now able to look back at the Titanic. I saw the vessel was sinking, and she went down with a volley of loud explosions caused, in my opinion, by the air breaking up the decks, and possibly the rending of the watertight compartments, although some survivors have stated they were caused by the boilers exploding.

"The lights of the vessel had disappeared one by one as she sank, and I continued to swim in the

darkness. Suddenly I saw before me what proved to be an upturned lifeboat of the Titanic, with a number of people standing on it. I swam up to this, and got hold of it, while there were shouts of 'Look out you will swamp us'. Naturally I did not pay much attention to these, but managed to draw myself up to the side of it. I was wearing a lifejacket, which kept me well up in the water, while the overturned boat was low down......

The boat that he had reached was Collapsible B, which had been washed off the ship by the wave and was still upside down. In addition to the people he could see on the keel of the boat, Harold Bride, the junior wireless operator, was under the boat, having grabbed one of the fixed oarlocks as the boat was swept over the side and found himself underneath. He later dived out and climbed on to the stern, where he joined Jack Thayer, who had jumped over the side as the ship started its final plunge; at that point the forefunnel had fallen into the water causing a 'tidal wave', which had driven Thayer up against the boat and thrust it and him away from the ship. Towards the bows of the boat was Second Officer Lightoller, who had been on the roof of the officer's quarters as the ship stood on end. He dived out forward but was forced against a ventilator and sucked down; then a rush of air from below blew him clear and he too was washed up against the collapsible.

Algy hauled himself onto the upturned boat, where his arrival has been described; *'Then came A.H. Barkworth, a Yorkshire Justice of the Peace. He wore a great fur coat over his lifebelt, and this daring arrangement surprisingly helped buoy him up. Fur coat and all, he too clambered on to the upturned collapsible, like some bedraggled, shaggy animal.'*

He continues his own story, *"....By the time I had got to it I could hear the cries and groans of the drowning people. It was terrible to hear them. We could do nothing for them, for we were helpless on the drifting overturned boat, which was swept away by the strong current from the struggling people in the water. If it had been taken towards them there is no doubt it would have been swamped. Several did manage to swim to the boat and climbed on to it..."*

One of those who climbed on was Colonel Gracie, who had been on the roof of the officers quarters with Lightoller, but instead of jumping he hung on and was sucked down with the ship. Eventually he fought his way to the surface and, like Algy, swum away supported by bits of wreckage until he came across the upturned boat. By that time the number on the boat was becoming a problem and his welcome was no more cordial than had been Algy's. Colonel Gracie recounts that he met with a 'doubtful reception' but hauled himself aboard and adopted 'a reclining position'; this was close to where Algy was crouching.. Another dozen or so followed until there were over thirty people on the unstable 'raft', after which members of the crew refused to allow any aboard, advising those clinging to wreckage nearby to ' hang on to what they had '.

The ship had gone down at 2.20. Algy's watch had stopped. It was impossible to keep track of time when the senses were numb with cold. The moaning cries of those in the water, which Algy and others found so distressing, died down. It is difficult to say how long it took but in the icy water survival time was bound to be short. There had been the initial thrill [a word much used in the press accounts] of the escape from the ship but the night on the boat was a patient struggle for survival in which there was little initiative. Those in the bow and stern used planks as paddles with little effect. Some shouted ' Boat Ahoy' in a hopeless effort to attract help but were soon persuaded to save their breath.

Occasionally someone saw a light which briefly raised hopes. At sometime one of the seaman suggested that they should pray and began a 'roll call' of denominations; they settled for the Lord's Prayer. Worst of all was the cold; their clothes were soaked, the air temperature was only just above freezing and every now and then, as Algy tells, water slopped over the keel numbing hands, feet and any other part of the body in contact with the boat.

".. There were over twenty of us crouching on either side of the keel and our limbs were becoming paralysed by the coldness of the water. We decided it would be better to stand up, and so one by one we stood up very gently so that our frail craft was not overbalanced. Even in this position the water washed over our ankles with the least movement. During the weary night two died and one slipped off into the sea, when it began to get up in the morning. One body was subsequently taken on to the

Carpathia, and it was buried at sea.

As daylight broke we could see the Carpathia about three miles away, although we could not do anything to move in her direction. I then discovered that there was one of the Titanic's officers also on the overturned lifeboat, and he blew his whistle and we shouted loudly, and, when one of the Titanic's lifeboats got within hailing distance, he ordered it to stand by, and we were taken off. Two of the Titanic's boats came alongside and we were got off in perfect order, commencing at one end of the submerged boat and finishing at the other. This will account for the reports that have been circulated that several of the boats contained more men than women. In the case I have mentioned at least thirty men were taken from our boat. The Titanic's lifeboats were already full when we got into them, and there would be about sixty people in the lifeboat in which I arrived alongside the Carpathia.."

Algy's estimate was low. The boat was in fact carrying over seventy people and was dangerously overloaded. This made it sluggish and difficult to handle in a rising sea and gusting wind. Soaking wet and frozen stiff, the survivors from the collapsible sat squeezed together on the thwarts. Those already in the boat were at least fairly dry and lent blankets or coats. Algy shared a steamer rug with a seaman on one side and Colonel Gracie on the other, while the Colonel tried vainly to resuscitate the dead member of the crew, whose body Second Offiicer Lightoller had lifted into the boat before stepping off the collapsible. They put the rug over their heads and huddled together to get some warmth.

CUNARDER "CARPATHIA" LEAVING MESSINA

Lightoller, equally cold and exhausted, had a further test of the stamina and seamanship that he had displayed continuously over the past hours. Draped in a hooded cape provided by a woman passenger, he coaxed the wallowing lifeboat towards the Carpathia, while Captain Rostron manoeuvred to bring the lifeboat into the lee of his ship. To those in the boat it seemed to take an interminable time but at about 8.30, more than six hours after the Titanic had sunk, Number 12 lifeboat lay alongside Carpathia, the last of the lifeboats to reach safety. To Algy, who was near to exhaustion, the transfer to the rescue ship was a testing ordeal....

" The women were sent up in slings and the children in coal bags, and the men climbed up the rope ladder. The latter was a difficult feat after the experience we had gone through, and with the rolling of the ship.

Once on board we were received with the greatest kindness, and no words of mine can speak too highly of the kindness of the captain, officers, doctors and crew alike. I am glad to note that some 4,500 dollars collected on the Carpathia have been devoted to recognising their great kindness to the survivors."

Many of the survivors from the upturned boat had to be treated for frostbite. Harold Bride was particularly affected in the ankles and feet since, in the earlier part of the night, someone had been lying on his legs restricting the circulation. Algy had frostbite in the fingers and was also deeply distressed, as Colonel Gracie his neighbour in the lifeboat later wrote,' *the combination of cold and the awful scenes of suffering which he had witnessed deeply affected A.H. Barkworth, whose tender heart is creditable to his character'.* As for the Colonel himself....*I mounted the ladder and, for the purpose of testing my strength, I ran up as fast as I could and experienced no difficulty or feeling of exhaustion....*

While the casualties were treated in the ship's dispensaries and fitted with dry clothes provided by Carpathia's crew and passengers, Captain Rostron hoisted most of Titanic's lifeboats on deck and turned the rest loose. He then hauled in the rope ladders which had hung along the ship's side and cruised slowly through the area but found only debris. That done he set sail for New York, where news of the disaster had already broken .

News of the sinking had been flashed from Cape Race and an extra edition of the New York Tribune, issued at 4.30 A.M. carried the headlines , 'TITANIC SINKING IN MID-OCEAN; HIT GREAT ICEBERG'. The report went on to list some of the 'noted' people on board and pictured the liner and its 'sumptuous' dining saloon. It also struck a slightly optimistic note, stressing the number of ships in the area which would be in a position to lend assistance. A news flash from New York also reached England and at breakfast on the same morning Algy's mother and sisters were alarmed by a short column on page 4 of their Hull Daily Mail headed, 'TITANIC SINKING - In Mid-Atlantic - Frantic Wireless Messages - Women Taken Off In Lifeboats'.

In Hull the next morning,Tuesday 16th, the headlines told of TITANIC'S DOOM, the 'Feared Loss of 1,500 Souls' and ' Rumoured Swamping Of Lifeboats'. To confuse matters his mother received the message announcing, *'All Well - Algy'.* The family rightly decided that this had been sent earlier and waited anxiously for news. In the meantime Carpathia had been wirelessing the names of the survivors that had been picked up. Conditions were difficult and Cape Race reported that they were having problems with the spelling, so that a first incomplete list was published in the New York papers which did not include Algy. A revised list published on Wednesday included an entry, "Barthworth, A.H." Remembering the warning on spelling and recognising the peculiarites of English pronunciation, someone had added - "(Bathworth ?)". This was to be repeated each day until Saturday when "Barkworth, A.H." at last appeared.

Carpathia was not a fast ship and normally plied between New York and a round of ports in the Mediterranean, taking out tourists, bringing in immigrants or taking them back to visit their families. There were limited facilities for saloon passengers and she was now carrying over 700 additional passengers. In keeping with the mood of the survivors, Captain Rostron arranged for a clergyman on board to conduct a service in the passenger lounge, attended by those survivors who were well enough and Carpathia's own passengers and crew. During the ensuing passage to New York the survivors bedded down where they could, fed in relays and sat around on deck while they tried to talk themselves through their experiences. At some point on passage, when their names had finally been passed to Cape Race, the survivors were allowed to send messages to their families. Algy's message was as nearly succinct as his first and read, *"Am safe aboard Carpathia - Algy".* Reaching Tranby late on Thursday 18th April the cable was their first confirmation that he had indeed survived. Onboard the Cunarder he also bought a postcard of the ship but it was not presumably for posting. On it he noted for 'posterity'....

Put on Carpathia on the morning of April 15th 1912, ex 'Titanic', which sank at 2.20 am, lat:41.06 West, long: 5.14. Jumped overboard and got on to an overturned boat until rescued..

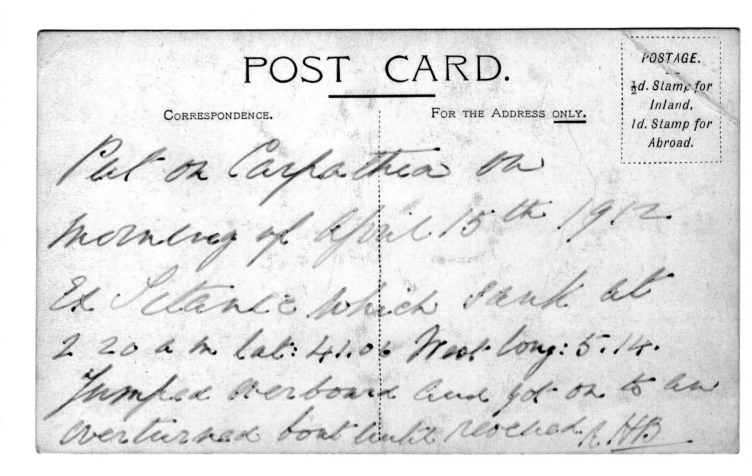

That same evening Captain Rostron brought Carpathia into New York. He rebuffed the press tugs, sent out to meet the ship, and dropped off the life boats at the White Star jetty before berthing. The survivors coming ashore are described as being 'dazed' and the press interviews that followed provided a mine of information and misinformation that was to continue for weeks and would contribute to years of controversy. Algy too was to be interviewed and the results cabled to the Hull Daily Mail, but first he took the opportunity to send his third message to Tranby. On the Friday his younger sister, Violet Pease, rang the newspaper in her excitement and said that he had cabled that morning to say that he was in a New York hotel and was safe and well. Dutifully the newspaper acknowledged *'the relief that this news had given his mother and sisters'* and that his *'many friends in Hull would read the news with great satisfaction'.* This report, genteel to the point of stuffiness, compared surprisingly with the banner headlines and sensational reporting of the "Sublime But Awful Spectacle" and "His Thrilling Escape In A Lifebelt" that appeared elsewhere on the same page.

In those early days it was Colonel Gracie, Algy's neighbour on the upturned Collapsible B and on the thwarts of Lifeboat Number 12, who did so much to keep the records straight. The Colonel was always dutiful, whether leading the unescorted ladies to the boats, helping with the loading and launching, or taking a last look round to see whether anyone needed help before running up the rope ladder to Carpathia. He now decided it was his duty to collate the survivors' stories while they were fresh in the mind. He therefore set about gathering information and personal accounts and hurried to complete his manuscript, although he became unwell. No sooner was it done than his luck ran out and he died on 4th December 1912, mainly, the doctors said, because of the toll which his experiences had taken of his constitution.

Great Uncle Algy was to be luckier. Having stayed his month in America, he recrossed the Atlantic and returned to Tranby House in mid-May, bringing with him his sea stained dress shirt and the fur coat that had helped him to survive. His frost-bitten fingers were recovering but were *still somwhat stiff*. His ordeal was not yet over and he was overwhelmed with congratulations and enquiries....*A sad side is the communications I receive from relatives asking for news of those who never returned. Of course I am unable to answer them.*

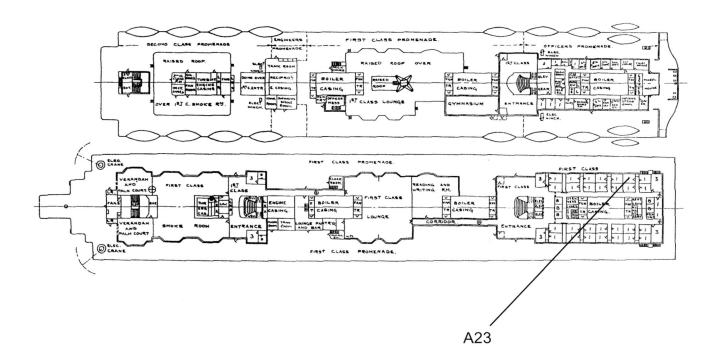

A23

A Deck, showing Algy's cabin, A23, the Smoking Room and the First Class Lounge
(The drawings shown here reproduced here by kind permission of Harland & Wolff)

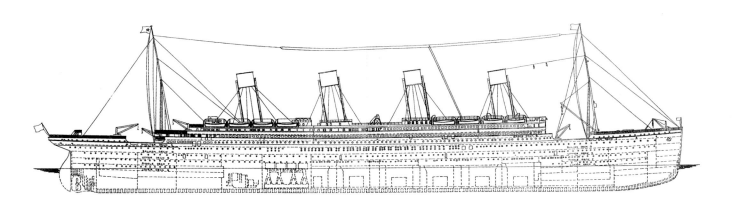

Epilogue

During the Great War of 1914 to 1918, Hull and its neighbourhood were the target of Zeppelin raids which claimed their share of killed and wounded and incurred the wrath of the citizens against the impotent defence provided by Govenrment. Algy predictably survived and, when in 1915 his mother died, Tranby House passed to Edmund, his elder brother, my grandfather. Edmund had his own house in Dorset and Algy continued to occupy Tranby, having reputedly bought the house for £4,000.

Here he continued to live with his unmarried sister and her companion, running a small farm and, like his brother and brother-in-law, performing his civic duty on the Council or on the Bench. From time to time he would tell the tale of the night on the upturned boat. Perhaps he did so once too often; the saltwater stained evening shirt was kept in a glass case, where it survived into the twenties until his niece, Dorothy, from vindictivenes or mischief, 'borrowed' it to clean her motorcycle and sidecar. Algy was angry but got over the loss and lived on at Tranby - as did the fur coat.

Twenty five years later, in June 1940, my father, serving with the Royal Engineers, returned from France, sailing from St Nazaire; he was fortunate and landed safely in England. The liner 'Lancastria', the next ship to leave, was not so lucky and was bombed and sunk with a loss of life proportional to that of the 'Titanic'.

Immediately on return, my father's Royal Engineer Unit had been sent first to Leeds and then to Darlington, where he was joined by my mother and from where together they paid their last visit to Tranby House. Here Algy's latest mechanical interest was a mill to grind the grain from his farm, which provided my father with a memorable bout of hay fever.

Algy's own Second World War experience began with the arrival of Hitler's bombers, bringing to Hull a more devastating version of the destruction caused by the Zeppelin raids of the Great War. He survived the second experience, as he had the first, but died in 1945 without seeing the second peace. He was the last of the Barkworth line to occupy Tranby House.

The fur coat passed to Eric Barkworth, his surviving nephew. Born in the Great War, Eric ('Bill' to his comrades) was serving in the SAS in 1945 and was to spend the post war years pursuing those responsible for the death of members of his Regiment - parachutists who had been captured after dropping into France and had been subsequently murdered, in accordance with one of Hitler's most infamous orders. After the war the coat was to make a further sea voyage, when Eric emigrated with his mother to Australia. There it was cut down to make her a cape for the cooler evenings. In turn it passed to Eric's wife, Lyn, with whom it was still residing in 1998 in a provincial town in Queensland, the last relic of that night on an upturned boat, where it had helped Algy to survive a disaster which cost over 1500 lives.

ork **Tribune.**

EW-YORK, MONDAY, APRIL 15. 1912.—TWELVE PAGES. • • • PRICE ONE CENT In City of New York, Jersey City and Hoboken ELSEWHERE, Two

R BARKWORTH'S RETURN

STRIKING STORY OF TITANIC DISASTER.

PT. SMITH'S MESSAGE to the LADIES

THE CRIES OF THE DROWNING.

(Exclusive to the "Daily Mail.")

H. Barkworth, J.P., of Tranby House, , has returned to his home after his ulous escape from death in the foundering Titanic.

ome persuasion, Mr Barkworth, who was hursday elected an East Riding County illor, consented to relate his experiences "Mail." In his thrilling story he brought t some new facts in this terrible disaster, ld exactly how his life was spared.

ere several outstanding incidents in the ive. For instance, when asked about the ts of the captain, Mr Barkworth replied : ast of Captain Smith I saw was when he urrounded by a crowd of crying ladies him many questions. "Go back to abins, ladies, and put on your lifebelts, me back to the boat deck. I assure here is no danger." I thought that d rather bad myself, added Mr Bark.

kworth also stated that soon after the nk the cries and screams of the ing people were terrible to hear.

ained that when he swam to an over- boat, and was about to clamber on it, f the survivors standing on it exclaimed, out; you will swamp us."

kworth also gave his version of the band ent, and what he heard the bandsmen g.

ANGING OVER SHIP'S SIDE.

nagnificence of the appointments of the g the social side of life on board, as briefly to by Mr Barkworth, served to throw rp contrast the terrible and sudden end Mr Barkworth was in the first-class room when the shock came.

r all the boats had gone everybody to be waiting for death on the doomed however, determined to leave the ship, ke a fight for my life in the water. I on to the top rail on the boat deck, and over, hung suspended by the side of the r the sea with one hand. I should say stance to the water was about now, for the vessel had su st that I thought she was going to t She had also sunk considerably in or ordinarily the distance to the have been nearly seventy feet. I f moments before dropping, fo to be full of chairs and othe overboard by the passenge I should hurt myself. kworth, in a reflective hat it was dangerous e side of the vessel, nk quickly, and they jump clear. He I swallowed no

VOLLEY OF

n I came to uld to ted would a large v imming wate age

CORRECTING AN IMPRESSION.

Mr Barkworth here stated he was anxious to correct the wrong impression caused in a hurried cable that he was in the water clinging to the overturned boat for six hours. That would have been a physical impossibility with the water at such a temperature. As indicated above, when he swam to this overturned boat he managed to climb on to it. He should think he was in the water and on this boat for over five hours. Hu watch had, of course, been stopped. Mr Bark worth explained that the boat had been launched wrong side up, which was fortunate for hir otherwise it would have been like the other b too far off for him to swim to it.

It was easy to picture the desolate spect the 20 to 25 men crouching and standing overturned boat. "By the time I had r he said, "I could hear the cries and the drowning people. It was terr them. We could do nothing for were helpless on the drifting o which was swept away by the str the struggling people in the been taken towards them t would have been swamped

DIED WITH E

"Several did manage climbed on to it. But of these died from e into the sea when it ing. One body w Carpathia, and As daylight apparently th not do anyth discovered officers blew hi one o distr ta

Mr Barkworth

well up in the water, while the overturned boat with the weight was low down. There were over twenty of us crouching on either side of the keel, and our limbs were becoming paralysed by the coldness of the water. We decided that it would be better to stand up, and so one by one we stood up very gently, so that our frail craft was not over-balanced. Even in this pos tion the water washed over our ankles with the least movement."

MR BARKWORTH HOME AGAIN.

HIS NARRATIVE OF THE TITANIC DISASTER.

Mr A. H. Barkworth, J.P., of Tranby House, Hessle, has returned to his home after his miraculous escape from death in the foundering of the Titanic.

After some persuasion, Mr Barkworth, who was on Thursday elected an East Riding County Councillor, consented to relate his experiences to the "Times." In his thrilling story he brought to light some new facts in this terrible disaster, and told exactly how his life was spared.

There were several outstanding incidents in the narrative. For instance, when asked about the last acts of the captain, Mr Barkworth replied : The last of Captain Smith I saw was when he was surrounded by a crowd of crying ladies asking him many questions. "Go back to your cabins, ladies, and put on your lifebelts, and come back to the boat deck. I assure you there is no danger." I thought that sounded rather bad myself, added Mr Bark worth.

MR BARKWORTH'S THRILLING RESCUE.

JUMPED OVERBOARD AFTER THE BOATS HAD GONE.

SPECIAL INTERVIEW.

(REUTER'S SPECIAL TELEGRAM.)

NEW YORK.

Mr A. H. Barkworth, J.P. House, Hessle, said he was sitting State room when the vessel s lerk. He saw Mr W. T. S He described how the fore powdered ice. He note was listing heavily ice.

As Captain Smi to put on their hi cabin and C lifebelt and fur board. While he was swim wave passed over his about. he found a boat, helped on board. He clutched another man in. After tha being helped into the small boa Two men

MESSAGE FROM MR BARKW

Mrs Pease of Beverley informed the morning that the following wireless mes was received at Tranby House, Hessle, from brother, Mr Algernon H. Barkworth, J.P. who was on the Titanic:— "Am safe on board Car pathia. —Algie."

At 10 o'clock this morning Mr Barkworth private cabingram to his mother from a New York hotel, and stated he was now at a New York hotel and was safe and well. The relief by reassuring news was received with great sisters, Mrs Barkworth, his mother and his who will read this news with satisfaction in Hull

WHAT SAVED ONES SAY.

LIFEBOATS NOT FILLED; SHIP "MUST HAVE BROKEN."

(SPECIAL EX. TEL. CALEDON.)

Edward Wheelton, a steward, said many women who refused to leave the them, and remaining on board went down at the same time, and most of them died from exposure as did two women in the water h Several hundred people were in the water and the children, some of whom were remarkably Calm. The women behaved wonderfully well. Dead Young.

BODIES COULD BE SEEN FLOATING

in the vicinity when daylight broke, and then the women became somewhat frightened. Dead died together when daylight broke, and then Colonel J. J. Astor and Major Washington Dr Washington on the bridge of the sinking liner. last he saw of them they were standing on the bridge, with their arms extended to reach other and shoulders, assisted the loading of the boats, there officers, during the whole to reach each, I am con tent, Throughout the sinking of the ship's lent, said the doctor, that the

THE TITANIC BROKE IN TWO, why she sank I remember several time struck the rock fearfully the lifeboats were not completely filled for the fact that marc Quartermaster sel Officers struck

Tribune.

AY, APRIL 19, 1912.—SIXTEEN PAGES. • • PRICE ONE CENT In City of New York, Jersey City and Hoboken ELSEWHERE TWO CENTS.

AT 21-KNOT SPEED

S STORY OF TITANIC'S LOSS,

THRILLING DETAILS OF RESCUE

THE GIANT WHITE STAR LINER TITANIC.
REPORTED IN COLLISION WITH AN ICEBERG ON HER FIRST TRIP TO NEW YORK.
THE ALLAN LINE STEAMER VIRGINIAN IS STEAMING TO THE TITANIC'S ASS

ALIAN GROCER SLAIN AS LETTER THREATENED

lled from Table by Self-St

EXTRA EDITION 4:30

TITANIC SINKING IN MID-OCEAN; GREAT ICE

Morning Blurred Women Being Liners R rilled Me

ITH TITANIC SURVIVORS, ARRIVING AT HER DOCK LAST NIGHT.
THREE OF THE TITANIC'S LIFEBOATS, FROM WHICH WERE RESCUED SOME 150 PAS
E ILL-FATED LINER. THESE BOATS HAD TO BE LOWERED AND TOWED AWAY BEFORE
IA COULD BE BROUGHT ALONGSIDE THE CUNARD PIER.
(Photo copyright by American Press Association.)

Mrs. Straus Refused to Leave Her Husband; Major Butt and Colonel Astor Together as Steamer Sank—Captain Smith

Appendix

Survivors from Collapsible Lifeboat B

Passengers are shown in bold text.

Allen, Mr Ernest	Trimmer
Barkworth, Mr Algernon H.	**1st Class**
Bride, Mr Harold	Wireless Operator
Collins, Mr John	Scullion
Daly, Mr Eugene Patrick	**3rd Class**
Daniels, Mr Sidney Albert	Steward
Dorking, Mr Edward Arthur	**3rd Class**
Fitzpatrick, Mr Charles William N.	Mess Steward
Gracie, Colonel Archibald	**1st Class**
Harmer, Mr Abraham David Livshin	**3rd Class** *Died in Boat*
Hebb, Mr A.	Trimmer
Hurst, Mr Walter	Greaser
Joughin, Mr Charles John	Chief Baker
Judd, Mr Charles E.	Fireman
Lightoller, Mr Charles Herbert	Second Officer
Maynard, Mr J	Entree Cook
McGann, Mr James	Fireman
Mellors, Mr William John	**2nd Class**
Moss, Mr Albert Johan	**3rd Class**
O'Connor, Mr John	Trimmer
O'Keefe, Mr Patrick	**3rd Class**
Phillips, Mr John George	Wireless Operator. *may have Died in Boat*
Pregnall, Mr George	Greaser
Senior, Mr Harry	Fireman
Snow, Mr Eustace Philip	Trimmer
Sunderland, Mr Victor Francis	**3rd Class**
Thayer, Mr John Borland Jr.	**1st Class**
Whiteley, Mr Thomas	Saloon Steward

As no records were kept as to who was placed in each lifeboat, it has only been possible to assemble the above list from a number of different sources such as personal accounts and reports of the incidents of that night.

Colonel Gracie records correspondence with a John Hagan (not the fireman of that name), who wrote to him about his experiences on the upturned boat, and described himself as 'working his passage'.

References

'A Night To Remember'. By Walter Lord. Published by Penguin Books in 1978.
    First published by Longman's, Green & Co in 1956.
'Titanic'. By Colonel Archibald Gracie. First published in 1913 under the title, 'The Truth About The Titanic'. Republished by Alan Sutton 1985.
'Titanic.Destination Disaster'. By John P.Eaton & Charles A. Haas. Published by Patrick Stephens Ltd in 1987
'Titanic'. By Thomas E. Bonsall. Distributed by Gallery Books, an imprint of W.H.Smith inc.
    Published in USA by Bookman Publishing in 1987.
Family papers:-
    Postcards
    Reports published in the Hull Daily Mail in May 1900 and in April and May 1912.
    Reports published by the New York Tribune in 1912.

Index

The Luck to Survive

A Family Experience of Disaster and War
1912-1920

Lieutenant Colonel Brian Edwards R.M.

£34.95 Case Bound Edition
ISBN 1-902074-04-1

24.95 Perfect Bound Edition
ISBN 1-902074-07-6

This book links together the stories of ten members of the author's family and that of his wife, drawing extensively on personal diaries, letters and accounts, hitherto unpublished.

During World War One they served in various regiments, including the Royal Artillery, the East Yorks, the Duke of Wellington,s Rgt., the Welsh Rgt., the Honourable Artillery Company, the 20th London Rgt., the Artist Rifles. One was even a member of the Imperial Russian Army. Between them they were to take part in campaigns from Flanders to Gallipoli, Salonica to the Carpathians, Egypt to Palestine and after the war from Ireland to Iraq. Against all the odds, nine of the ten were to survive.

However, the story begins with the loss of the Titanic and the dramatic survival of Algernon Barkworth, who made his escape on an upturned collapsible life boat.

This extensively researched and detailed work provides a fascinating insight to the major campaigns of World War One as well as the most famous shipping disaster in history.

This book is available from your book shop or direct from **Gordons Publishing** G14-15 Grays Antique Centre, 1-7 Davies Mews Davies Street, London W1Y 1AR. England.